**Hawys Morgan**

American English

Student's Book
with Digital Pack

1

# Our Book

# Hello

Listen. Point. Draw.

**Welcome** Vocabulary Presentation: hello, goodbye, thank you, Daniel, Sofia, Hug, Hummy

Extra

Color.

Extra
Draw.

Match.  Say.

Extra
Color.

# 1 Our Rainbow

▶ 🎧 03 Listen. 👆 Point. 🎵 Sing.

Stick. Circle.

Extra

Find.

Point.  Say.  Color.

Trace.

**Listen.**  **Point.** **Color.**

**1**

**2**

**3**

**4**

**Extra** Find.

Match.  Follow.  Say.

 Color.

Extra

Circle.

Say.  Trace.  Color.

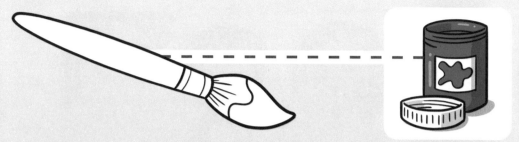

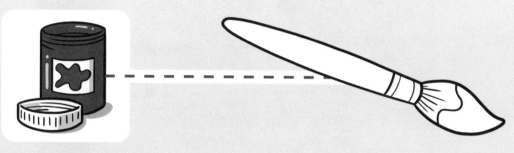

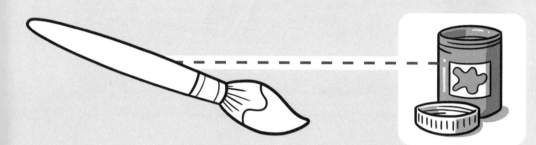

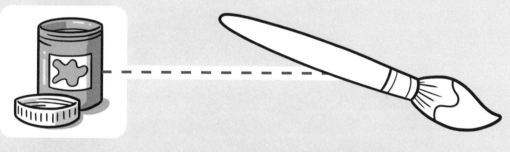

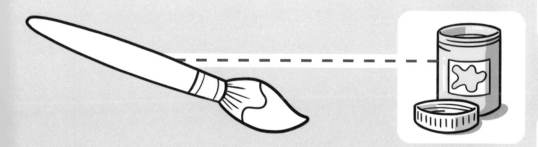

**Think.**  **Circle.**  **Draw.**

Extra

Mime.

# 2 Our Classroom

▶ 🎧 05 Listen. 👆 Point. 🎵 Sing.

Stick. Draw.

Extra
Trace.

Point.  Say.  Match.

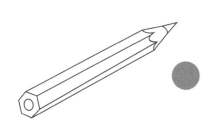

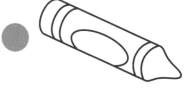

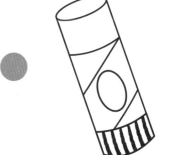

Extra

Color.

**Listen.**  **Point.**  **Color.**

**1**

**2**

**3**

**4**

Find.

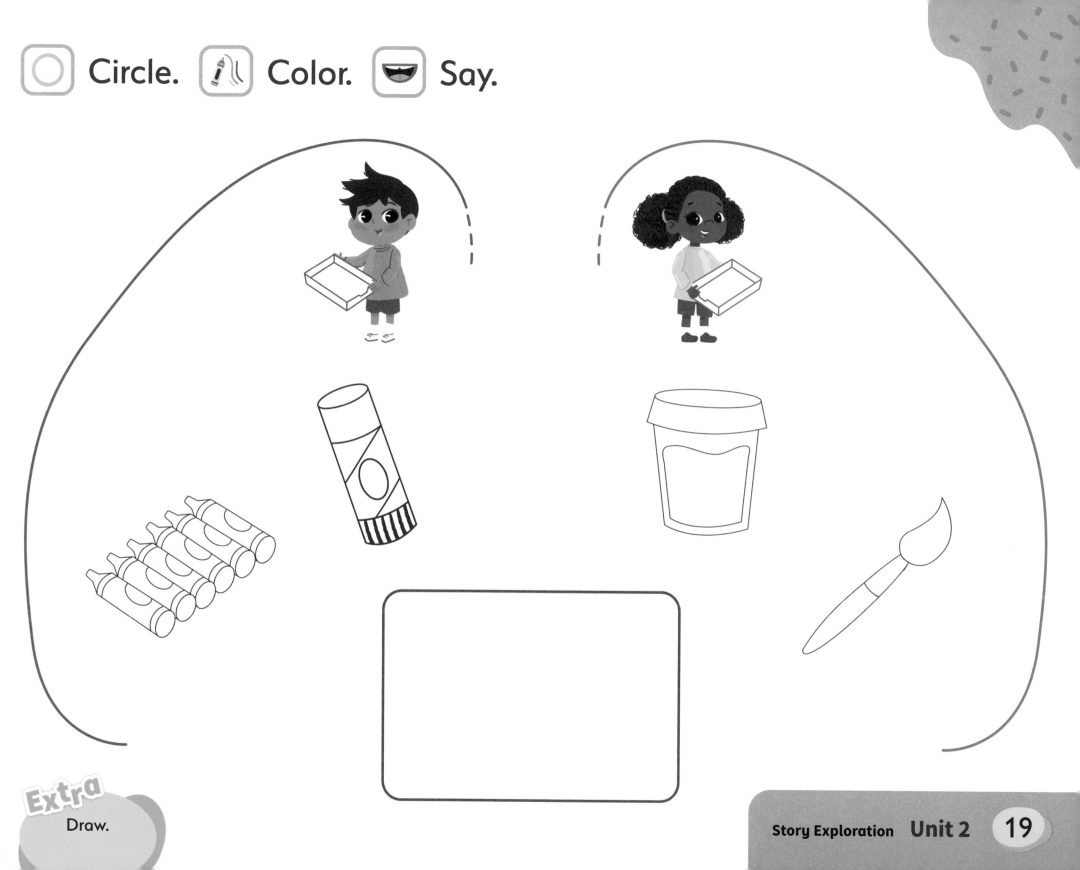

Circle. Color. Say.

Extra
Draw.

Watch.  Say.  Match.

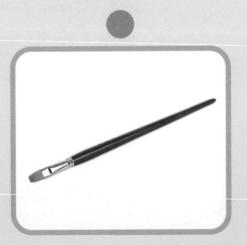

Extra

Count.

Say.  Circle.

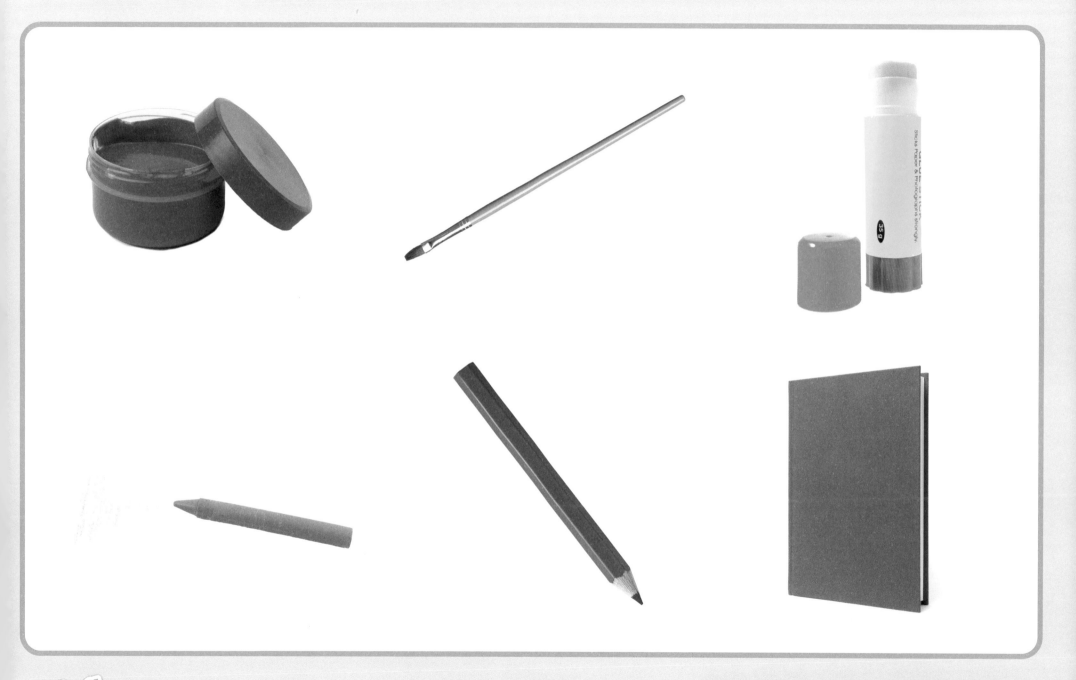

**Review:** This is my (book). **Unit 2** 21

Think.  Circle.  Say.

22 Unit 2 **Well-being:** I feel like people are friendly.

 Find.

# 3 Our Feelings

  Listen.  Point.  Sing.

Stick. Draw.

Extra
Color.

Point.  Say.  Circle.

**Listen.**  **Point.**  **Color.**

1

2

3

4

Extra

Find.

 Circle.  Say.

Color.

Watch.  Say.  Match.

Extra

Mime.

**Say.**  **Circle.**

# Think. ✏️ Draw. 🖍️ Color.

**Unit 3** **Well-being:** I feel like I am doing well.

Extra
Say.

# 4 Our Families

  Listen.  Point.  Sing.

Extra

Color.

Stick. Draw.

Extra
Trace.

**Point.**  **Say.**  **Circle.**

**Listen.**  **Point.**  **Color.**

**1**

**2**

**3**

**4**

Extra
Find.

Match.  Say.

Extra

Count.

**Watch.**  **Say.**  **Match.**

Extra

Mime.

**Say.**  **Trace.**  **Color.**

Think. Draw.

Extra

Color.

# 5 Our Bodies

Listen. Point. Sing.

Stick. Circle.

Extra

Color.

Point.  Say.  Circle.

Mime.

**Listen.**  **Point.**  **Color.**

**1**

**2**

**3**

**4**

Extra

Trace.

Circle.  Say.  Color.

1

2

**Extra**
Mime.

**Watch.**  **Say.** **Match.**

Extra

Circle.

 Circle.  Mime.

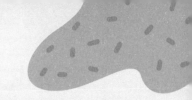

Count.

**Think.**  **Color.**  **Draw.**

Extra

Mime.

# 6 Our Clothes

▶️ 🎧13 Listen. 👆 Point. 🎵 Sing.

Stick. ◯ Circle.

48 Unit 6 Vocabulary Practice

Extra

Count.

**Point.**  **Say.**  **Match.**

Listen.  Point. Color.

Extra

Find.

 Circle.  Say.  Trace.

Watch.  Circle.  Say.

  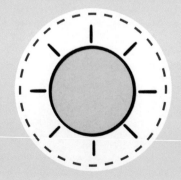 

 Extra

Color.

**Say.**  **Circle.**  **Color.**

**Extra**

Draw.

**Think.**  **Color.**  **Say.**

Extra

Count.

# 7 Our Pets

🎧 Listen. 👆 Point. 🎵 Sing.

Stick. Circle.

Extra
Draw.

Point.  Say.  Circle.

Count.

**Language Presentation:** I have / don't have a (bird). **Unit 7** 57

**Listen.**  **Point.** **Color.**

**Extra**

Trace.

Trace.  Say.  Circle.

Extra
Color.

Watch.  Count. ◯ Circle.

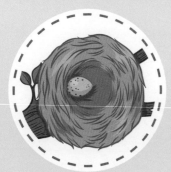   

Extra
Draw.

Say.  Match. 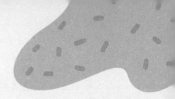 Circle.

Extra

Mime.

Think.  Say.  Circle.

Extra

Count.

# 8 Our Lunch

▶ 🎧 17 Listen.  👆 Point.  🎵 Sing.

Extra
Color.

Stick. Circle.

Extra
Draw.

Point.  Follow.  Say.

Draw.

**Language Presentation:** I like / don't like (apples). **Unit 8** 65

**Listen.**  **Point.**  **Color.**

**1**

**2**

**3**

**4**

Extra

Count.

Draw.  Say.  Circle.

Color.

Watch.  Say.  Match.

Extra

Circle.

Draw.  Say.  Circle.

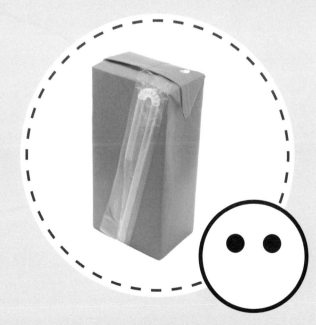

Count.

Think. Draw. Color.

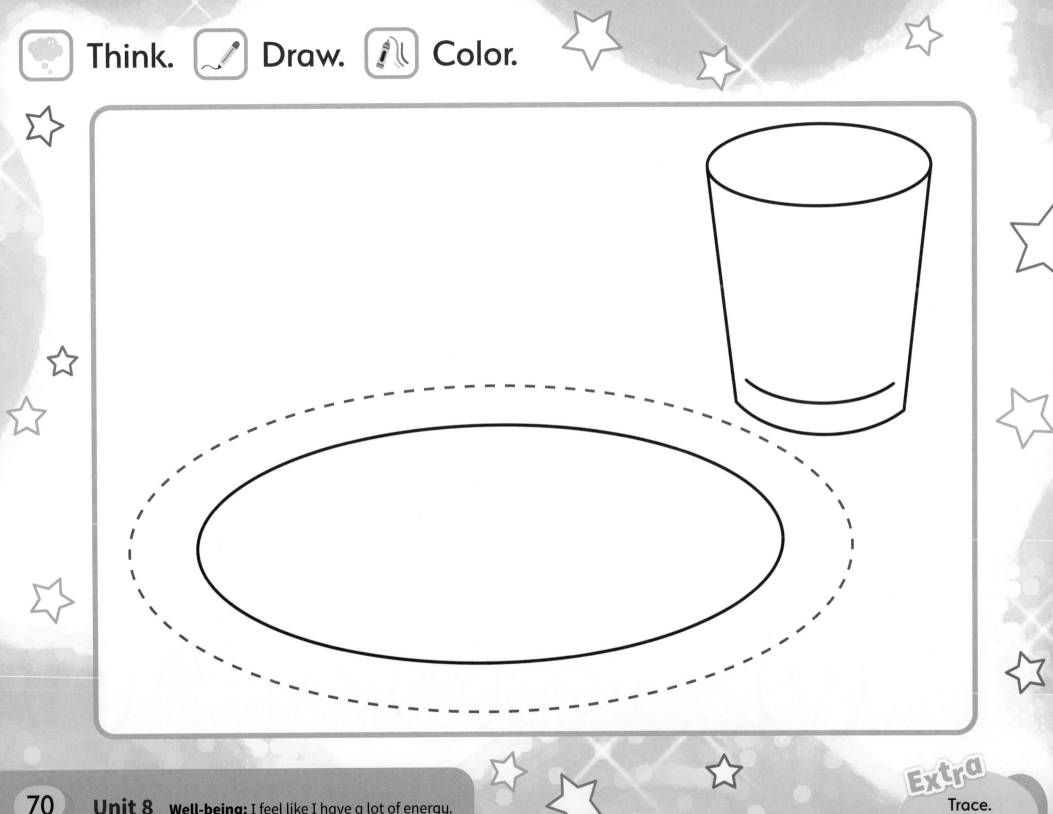

**Well-being:** I feel like I have a lot of energy.

Extra

Trace.

# 9 Our Toys

Listen. Point. Sing.

Stick. Circle.

Extra

Draw.

Point.  Say.  Circle.

Count.

**Language Presentation:** What's that? It's a (ball). **Unit 9** 73

Listen.  Point.  Color.

**1**

**2**

**3**

**4**

Extra
Circle.

Say.  Match.  Color.

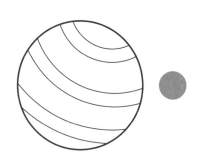

**Watch.**  **Trace.**  **Color.**

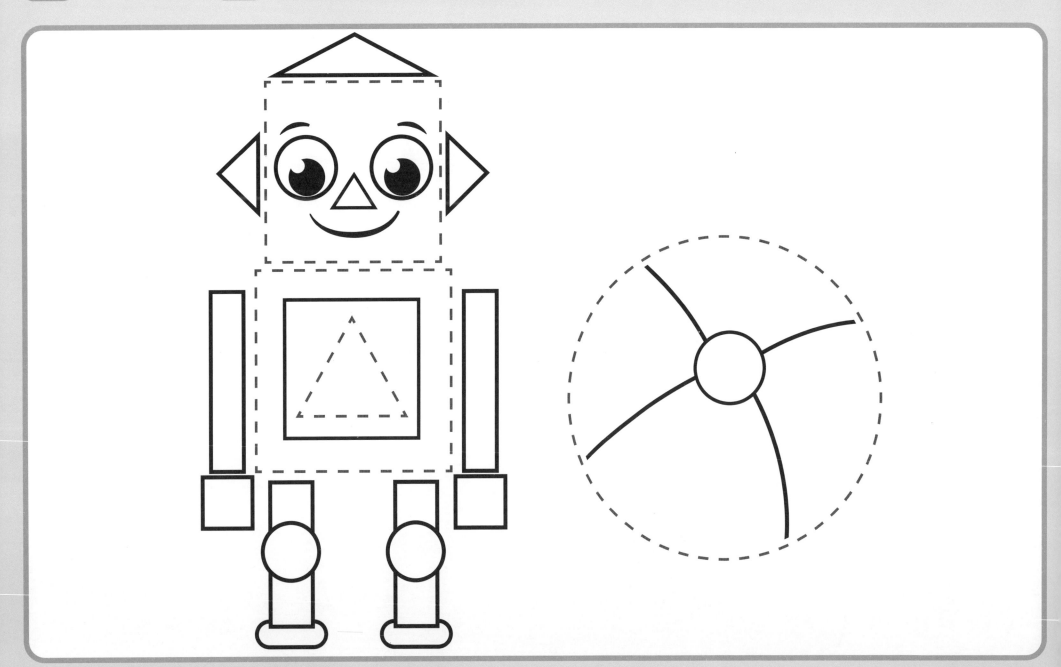

Extra

Count.

**Say.**  **Circle.**

**Extra**

Mime.

**Think.**  **Draw.**

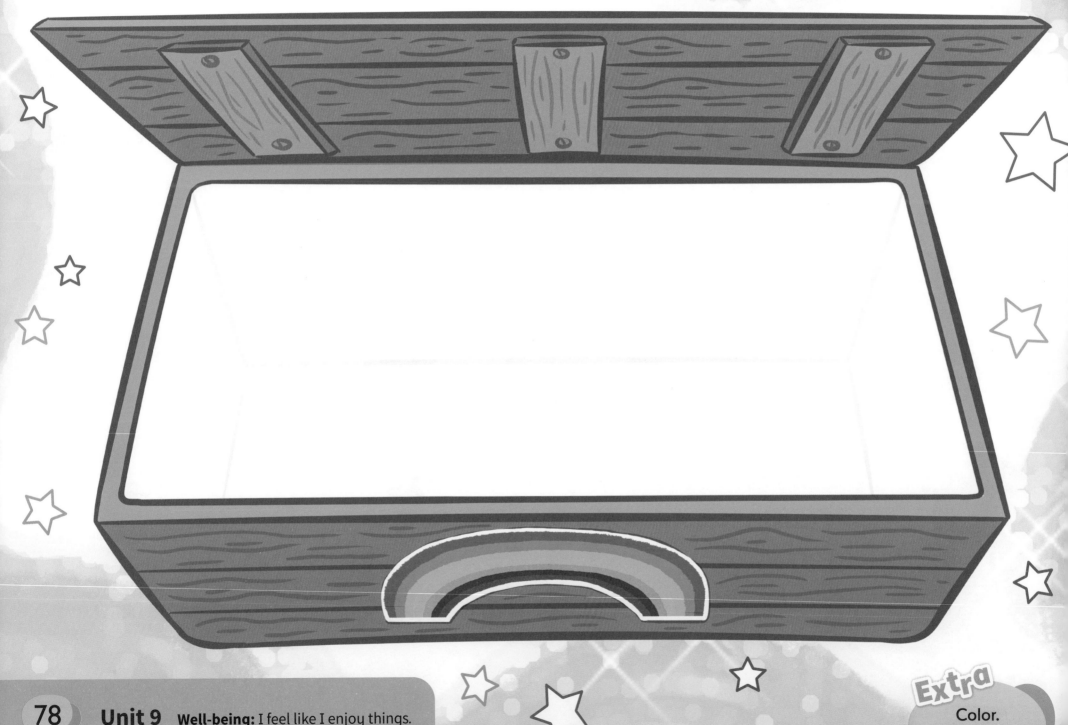

**Extra**

Color.

Listen.  Follow.  Say.

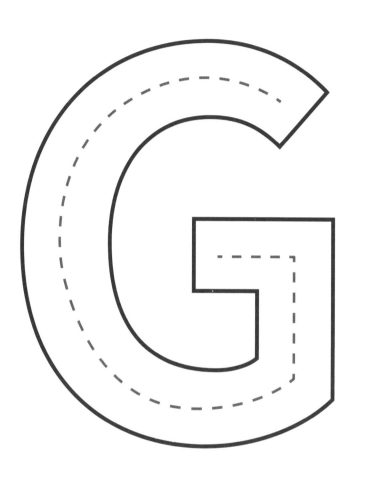
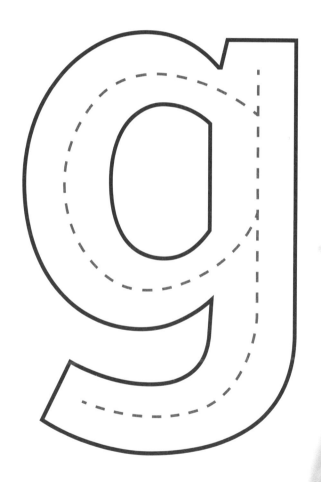

**Listen.**  **Follow.**  **Say.**

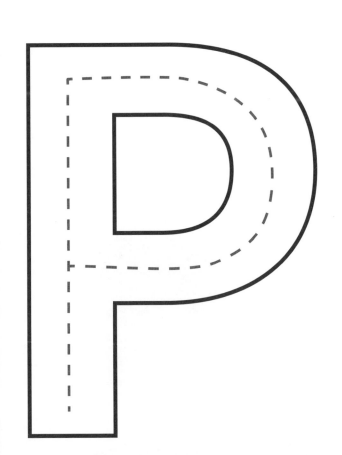

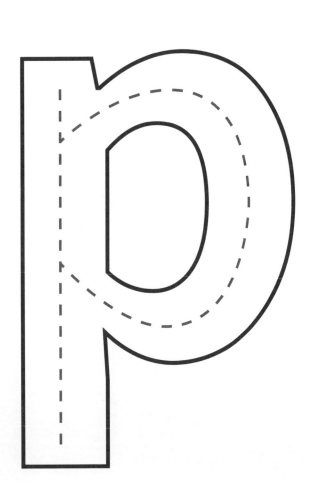

Extra

Color.

Listen.  Follow.  Say.

Color.

Listen.  Follow. Say.

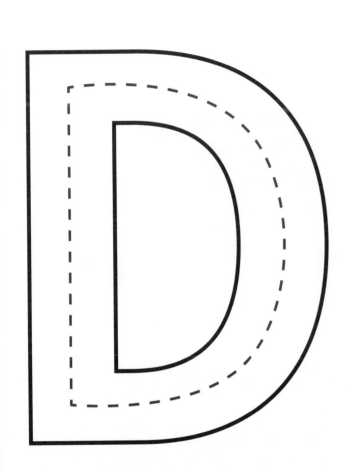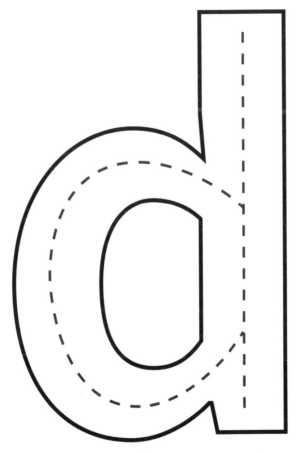

Extra
Color.

Listen.  Follow.  Say.

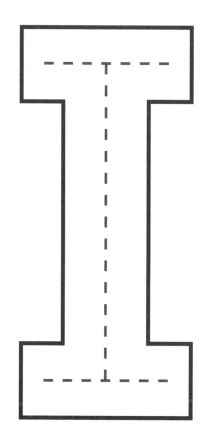

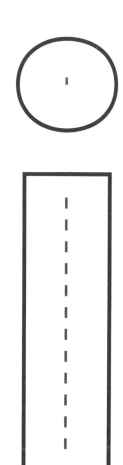

Color.

**Listen.**  **Follow.**  **Say.**

Extra

Color.

Listen.  Follow.  Say.

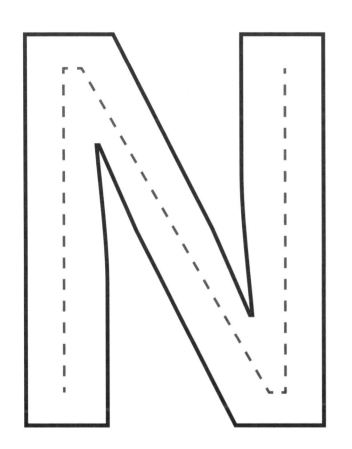

Color.

Nn **Sounds** 85

**Listen.**  **Follow.**  **Say.**

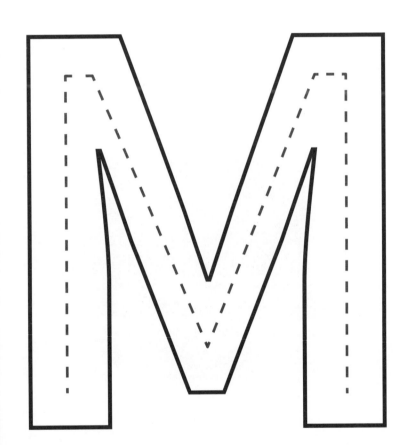

Extra

Color.

**Listen.**  **Follow.**  **Say.**

Color.

**Count.**  **Say.**  **Circle.**

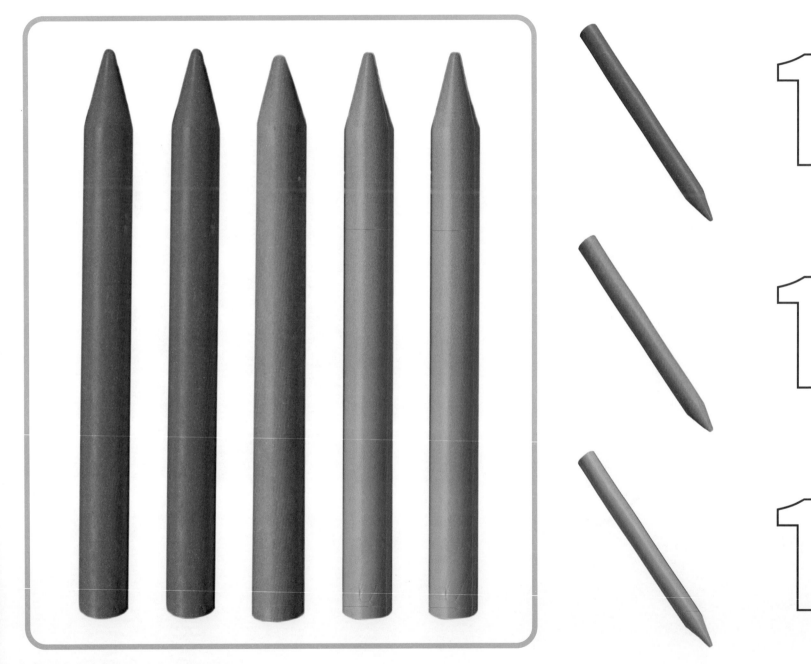

1    2

1    2

1    2

Extra
Color.

**Count.**  **Say.**  **Trace.**

31

**Extra**

Color.

Count.  Say.  Draw.

Extra
Color.

Count.  Say.  Circle.

Extra
Color.

Count.  Color.  Trace.

1 = 2 = 3 = 4 = 5 = 6 =

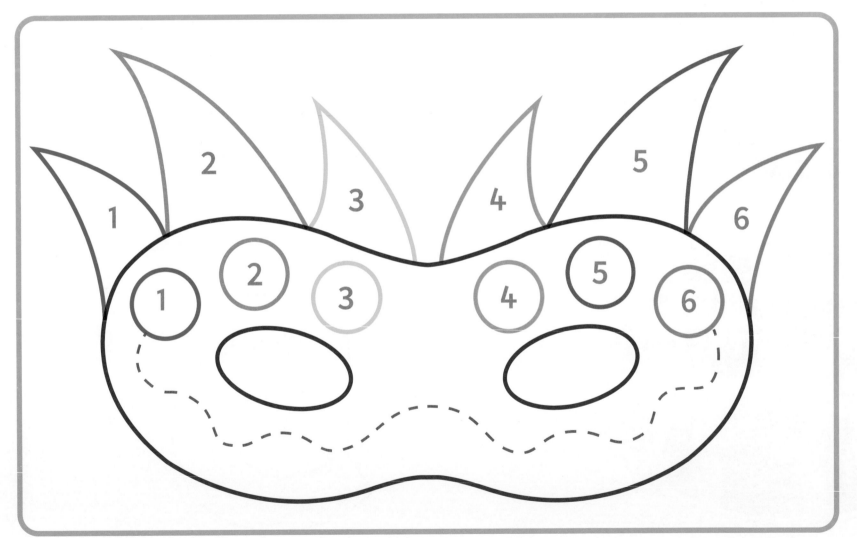

Extra

Color.

Say.  Count.  Circle.

Color.

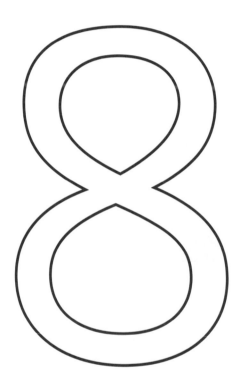

**Circle.**  **Count.**  **Say.**

37

Color.

**Count.**  **Draw.**  **Circle.**

38

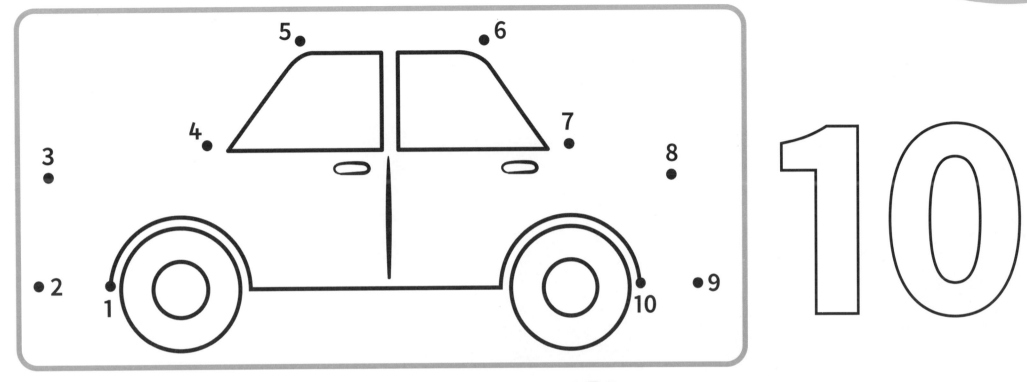

**10**

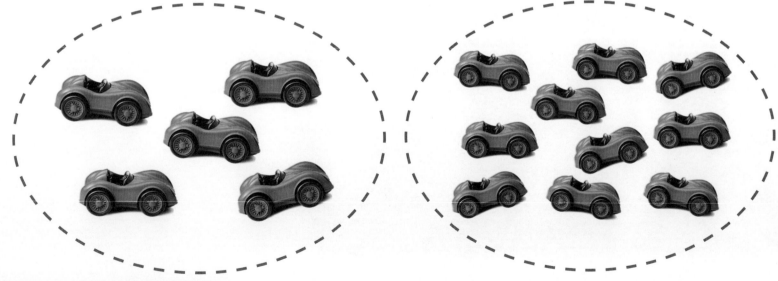

Color.

# Stickers

## Welcome  Page 5

## Unit 1  Page 8

## Unit 2  Page 16

# Stickers

## Unit 3  Page 24

## Unit 4  Page 32

# Stickers

## Unit 5 Page 40

## Unit 6 Page 48

## Unit 7 Page 56

# Stickers

## Unit 8  Page 64

## Unit 9  Page 72